CW01189438

1 MONTH OF FREE READING

at

www.ForgottenBooks.com

By purchasing this book you are eligible for one month membership to ForgottenBooks.com, giving you unlimited access to our entire collection of over 1,000,000 titles via our web site and mobile apps.

To claim your free month visit: www.forgottenbooks.com/free922280

* Offer is valid for 45 days from date of purchase. Terms and conditions apply.

ISBN 978-0-260-01393-4
PIBN 10922280

This book is a reproduction of an important historical work. Forgotten Books uses state-of-the-art technology to digitally reconstruct the work, preserving the original format whilst repairing imperfections present in the aged copy. In rare cases, an imperfection in the original, such as a blemish or missing page, may be replicated in our edition. We do, however, repair the vast majority of imperfections successfully; any imperfections that remain are intentionally left to preserve the state of such historical works.

Forgotten Books is a registered trademark of FB &c Ltd.
Copyright © 2018 FB &c Ltd.
FB &c Ltd, Dalton House, 60 Windsor Avenue, London, SW19 2RR.
Company number 08720141. Registered in England and Wales.

For support please visit www.forgottenbooks.com

No. 7.

DREW

STUDENTS'

HAND-BOOK

1904=1905

PRESENTED BY THE

Young Men's Christian Association

OF

DREW THEOLOGICAL SEMINARY

Compliments of Drew Theological Seminary Library

•

PUBLISHED BY THE
YOUNG MEN'S CHRISTIAN ASSOCIATION
OF DREW THEOLOGICAL SEMINARY,
MADISON, NEW JERSEY.
MCMIV

Contents.

	PAGE.
Advertisements	65
Athletics	32
Browning Club	36
Chapel Preachers	28
Daily Programme	48
Devotional Meetings	27
Drew Missionaries	14
Drew Settlement	9
Drew Quartette	31
Faculty	4
Fellowships	31
General Information	33
Greeting	3
Historical Sketch	5
Lectures and Addresses	29
Library	10
Madison Churches	40
Madison Public Library	39
Madison Y. M. C. A.	38
Mail Service	46
M. E. Churches of New York	40
Missions	12
Phi Alpha Literary Society	38
Places of Interest in Brooklyn	45
Places of Interest in New York	42
Prominent Churches in New York	41
Self Help	32
Seminary Buildings	7
Seminary Calendar	49
Shaksperean Club	37
Student Charges	31
Suggestions	35
Time-table of Trains	47
Y. M. C. A. Constitution	19
Y. M. C. A. Officers and Committees	18
Y. M. C. A. Treasurer's Report	26

Greeting.

The Young Men's Christian Association of Drew extends to every man in seminary the hand of kindly greeting.

We are glad to welcome the new men, and trust that they may at once recognize the honest manliness and sterling Christainty of the "Drew brotherhood," and feel the cheerful cordiality with which we greet them.

The old men can never be forgotten. "Dear old Drew," around which their memory fondly lingers, loves them still, and gives them "God speed" in their life-work.

The Drew men everywhere, old men and new, are one body, and the head is the man Christ Jesus.

GEO. P. DOUGHERTY,
WM. M. NESBIT,
W. S. JACKSON,
E. W. BYSHE,
Committee.

The Faculty of Drew Theological Seminary.

The Rev. Henry A. Buttz, D. D., LL. D., President, and Professor of New Testament Exegesis.

The Rev. Samuel F. Upham, D. D., LL. D., Professor of Practical Theology.

The Rev. Robert W. Rogers, M. A., Ph. D. (Leipzig), D. D., LL. D., F. R. G. S., Professor of Hebrew and Old Testament Exegesis.

The Rev. Charles F. Sitterly, B. D., Ph. D., S. T. D., Professor of Biblical Literature and Exegesis of the English Bible.

The Rev. Olin A. Curtis, M. A., S. T. D., Professor of Systematic Theology.

Walker V. Holt, Special Instructor in Elocution.

The Rev. John Alfred Faulkner, B. D., D. D., Professor of Historical Theology.

The Rev. Samuel G. Ayres, B. D., Librarian.

Historical Sketch of Drew.

The grounds of Drew Theological Seminary were once known as the "Forest," and comprised the estate of William Gibbons, who, with Aaron Ogden, his brother-in-law, formed a steamboat company, the rival of Livingston and Fulton. The mansion (now Mead Hall) was then the finest structure in this section of our country. And the stone wall along Madison avenue, the massive iron gates, and the stone porters' lodges are memorials of early grandeur. Dr. Faulkner's house and Asbury and Embury Halls belonged to the original estate.

Drew is one of the fruits of the centenary of Methodism in America. Daniel Drew, a wealthy New Yorker, purchased the estate and gave it to the church, erected four residences for professors, and supported the seminary for the first nine years of its existence, and would have provided for its permanent maintainance, but for his disastrous failure in 1876.

The seminary was chartered April 16, 1866, and formally opened November 6, 1867. The following are the names of the honored men who have served in its faculty. Rev. John McClintock, D. D., 1867-'70; Rev. B. H. Nadal, D. D., 1867-'70; Rev. H. A. Buttz, D. D., LL. D., 1868—; Prof. James Strong, D. D., 1868-'93; Rev. R. S. Foster, D. D., LL. D., 1869-'72; Rev. J. F. Hurst, D. D., LL. D., 1871-'80; Rev. D. P. Kidder, D. D., LL. D., 1871-

'81; Rev. John Miley, D. D., LL. D., 1871-'96; Rev. G. R. Crooks, D. D., LL. D., 1881-'97; Rev. S. F. Upham, D. D., LL. D., 1881—; Rev. C. F. Sitterly, Ph. D., S. T. D., 1891—; Rev. R. W. Rogers, Ph. D., D. D., LL. D., 1893—; Rev. O. A. Curtis, S. T. D., 1896—; Rev. J. A. Faulkner, D. D., 1897—.

The presidents of Drew have been Dr. McClintock, 1867; Dr. Foster, 1870; Dr. Hurst, 1872; Dr. Kidder, 1880; and Dr. Buttz, 1880. Drs. Foster and Hurst left the presidency to assume the episcopal dignity, and Dr. Kidder, to become Secretary of the Board of Education. The other former members of the faculty gave their last service to the school, though Dr. Strong resigned before his death.

Thirty-six years of earnest labor by some of the best minds and hearts in Methodism have given Drew Seminary a character distinctively its own; and the best thought of to-day is assimilated to the traditions of the past in a manner conducive to scholarship and evangelistic fervor.

The growth of the seminary has been sure and steady. The number of buildings has doubled; and to-day Drew stands in the forefront of the theological schools of our land. The increase in the size of the student body has filled all available room in the dormitories. The higher average ability and earnestness of the students has encouraged the faculty and trustees to devise means for advanced work. The result has been the adoption of the German Seminar method, which is greatly facilitated by the conveniences of the new Administration Building.

Moreover the establishment of the Drew Settlement in New York gives the men unexcelled opportunities for the study of applied Christianity among the needy of a great city.

To the loyalty of her alumni and the generosity of her friends Drew is indebted for the liberal gifts that have made such growth possible. That such contributions are being made shows how well the seminary has kept her charge and how firm a place she holds in the church.

The Seminary Buildings.

MEAD HALL

is the original mansion of the estate, and, until recently, was the chief point of seminary activity. It contains the offices of the President and Registrar, the Y. M. C. A. social room, the home of Dr. Curtis, rooms for eighteen students, and the Old Chapel, in which so many gracious meetings have been held, and which is ever the spiritual center of Drew life. A fine old building with its massive columns in front, its tiled floors, high ceilings, elegant mirrors, and huge inlaid doors; it is a fitting reminder of other days when it was much frequented by the celebrities of the time, for here Daniel Webster was wont to come, and here, too, Ward McAllister found his wife.

ASBURY HALL

stands about twenty feet north and a little east from Hoyt-Bowne Hall. It was a part of the old estate and was remodeled in 1867 to meet the needs of seminary work. It contains the home of Mr. Ayres, the stationery store, the tailor shop, the barber shop, the laundry agency, and rooms for forty students.

EMBURY HALL

was remodeled at the same time as Asbury Hall. It is parallel to and east of Asbury. It contains the dining hall and steward's residence, also rooms for twenty-five students. The heating plant for the seminary buildings adjoins.

CORNELL LIBRARY,

the gift of Mr. John B. Cornell and others, was built in 1896 at a cost of $90,000. It is one of the finest buildings on the campus and contains about 80,000 volumes exclusive of pamphlets, etc., making it the largest library in any American theological seminary.

HOYT-BOWNE HALL,

completed in 1895 at a cost of $100,000, is a brownstone and Pompeian brick building situated farthest south of all the seminary buildings. It is the joint gift of the late William Hoyt, formerly president of the board of trustees, and Samuel W. Bowne, now president of the board of trustees. This building is lighted by electricity and heated by steam. Besides rooms for 107 students, which are entirely furnished, inclusive of linen, by the ladies of the McClintock Association, it contains parlor and reception rooms, baths, and toilet rooms.

THE ADMINISTRATION BUILDING

was dedicated in 1899. It is built of granite and Harvard brick and cost over $100,000. The furnishings of this building are splendidly wrought and beautifully adapted to the needs of the work. The two friends of the seminary who made this gift have withheld their names. The picturesque Gothic Chapel is in this building, also lecture and seminar rooms for each member of the faculty. There is a reception-room on the first floor, while the basement contains cloak rooms, lavatory, and supply rooms. The building is equipped with steam heat and electric light.

The Drew Settlement in New York City.

The Drew Settlement in New York City, located just off the Bowery at 22 East Seventh Street, has just completed a very successful year's work.

A number of the Seniors have been employed under the direction of the Church Extension Society, in visiting the poor and neglected in their homes, in preaching and Sunday-school work, and thus they have come into personal contact with the people who need the Gospel most.

One of the most successful departments of the work has been the lecture course. The lecturers have been among the strongest talent available and have made the course both instructive and popular.

The Library.

The history of the Library is in one sense the history of the seminary. Mr. Drew gave $10,000, and with this first gift the library was begun in 1868.

The library of Dr. McClintock was purchased after his death, and soon after came the library of Rev. John D. Blain, at one time editor of the *California Christian Advocate.* The family of Dr. Thomas Carlton also presented many of his books.

In 1877, when Mr. Anderson Fowler secured through the Rev. William Arthur the library of the late Dr. George Osborne, the foundation of the present interesting collection of works relating to Methodism was begun. It has since been constantly growing, so that now the collection numbers over 8,000 titles. In 1882 steps were taken looking toward the erection of a building. This was accomplished and the building dedicated in 1888. It has been appropriately named the Cornell Library Building, in honor of Mr. John B. Cornell, the principal donor.

The first large gift after entering the new building was the library of Dr. Curry. Mr. William White, a generous donor, not only has given over 1,400 volumes, but founded our collection of early New Testament and other Greek manuscripts. This is now the largest collection of its kind in this country. For an account of other collections the reader is referred to the catalogues of 1896 and 1897.

The endowment of the alcoves of the library is as follows: The McClintock Association, $2,000. The Association gave also $2,000 which was expended in the purchase of books. The income of the endowment is for the purchase of reference books; the Nelson alcove, endowed by Mrs. Thomas Nelson and Mrs. Bennett, $2,000—devoted to the New Testament and the English Bible; the New York East Conference Alumni Association alcove, $2,000—devoted to Old Testament literature; the Fisk alcove, in memory of Gen. Clinton B. Fisk, $2,000—devoted to theology and philosophy; the Abbey alcove, in memory of Mrs. Abbey, who provided for it by will, $2,000—devoted to practical theology; the Thomas Irwin Cornell Memorial alcove, endowed by Mrs. F. A. Jayne, $2,000—devoted to secular history; Mrs. Jayne also gave $3,000 for the purchase of new books; the James McGee alcove, $2,000—named for the donor, devoted to church history; the Alumni Association Endowment Fund now amounting to over $1,000.

Its income is used for binding purposes. The Alumni Association has also purchased the library of the late Prof. James Strong, consisting of over 6,000 volumes and 4,500 pamphlets. Bishop Hartzell has undertaken the formation of a great collection on Africa and the African.

The family of the late Dr. James Strong has furnished a fund for the purchase of books relating to hymnology. The last large gift is the sum of $500 for the purchase of books on sociology.

The library is now the largest in Methodism, and also the largest of all the theological seminaries in the United States. On April 20, 1904, it contained over 81,000 volumes and more than 61,000 pamphlets.

An endeavor is made to purchase the best of the new books in the several departments of instruction. The library is more than a special theological library. The building is open from 8 a. m. to 5 p. m. daily. It is furnished with a card catalogue. The reading-room contains about 260 periodicals, and is open to all.

A library fine of two cents a day is imposed upon all books kept out of the library over three weeks.

Missions.

That the inscription on the pulpit in the Old Chapel, "The Field is the World," is more than empty sentiment is heroically proven in the lives of Drew men, not only in our own land, but in every foreign field. An earnest and intelligent missionary spirit exists among both faculty and students at Drew, proof of which may be seen in the list of Drew missionaries which follows.

Special attention is given to mission study in the department of practical theology, and in at least two other departments there is scope for elective reading courses on missions.

The remarkable work which Mr. Ayres has done in collecting a missionary library, with almost no funds at his disposal, is worthy of high praise. There are at present a total of 78 missionary magazines coming to the seminary library, while there are 6,500 pamphlets and 42,000 bound volumes of missionary literature in the library.

It is customary to have an optional class in mission study under the leadership of some student who is especially fitted for the work. Last year the leader was Mr. E. D. Soper, '05. The text-books were Graham's "Missionary Expansion since the Reformation" and Cary's "Japan and Her Regeneration."

There is a vigorous Volunteer Band in the seminary which holds meetings each week during the school year. The total membership for the past year was 22. The officers for the ensuing year are:

Leader—E. D. Soper.
Vice-Leader—V. M. McCombs.
Secretary—M. W. Beckwith.

Missionaries.

The following is a list of the former students of the seminary who have entered foreign missionary work:

AFRICA.

L. C. Burling, ex-'82, returned.
E. E. Pixley, '91, deceased.
Thomas Waite, '99, deceased.
R. E. Beetham, '01.
S. Gurney, ex-'89.
G. A. Baldwin, '94.

ARGENTINA.

D. W. Proseus, ex-'00.
J. G. Schilling, '93.

ARMENIA.

B. M. Krikorian, '90, massacred.

BULGARIA.

E. F. Lounsbury, '75, returned.
J. J. Economoff, '76.
Stephen Thomoff, '77.
Trico Constantine, '79.
M. D. Delchoff, '89.
P. C. Dunoff, '91.

BURMAH.

C. B. Hill, '96.
A. T. Leonard, '98.

CHINA.

S. D. Harris, '73, returned.
Thomas McClintock, '75, returned.
M. L. Taft, '77, returned.
James Blackledge, ex-'80, returned.
G. B. Smyth, '80, Field Secretary.
G. W. Woodall, ex-'81, returned.
G. E. Hartwell, '91.
T. A. Hearn, '94.

James Simister, '96.
H. F. Rowe, '97.
John Gowdy, '02.
Burton L. St. John, '02.
C. H. Johnson, '02, under appointment.

CHILI.

R. D. Powell, '85.
A. S. Watson, '01.

INDIA.

F. A. Goodwin, ex-'75, deceased.
W. E. Newlon, '75, deceased.
J. E. Robinson, ex-'75.
G. H. McGrew, '76, returned.
M. L. Banner, '77, retired.
P. M. Buck, '78.
C. L. Bare, '80.
S. S. Dease, '80.
F. L. Neeld, '81.
T. H. Oakes, '81, returned to England.
Niels Madsen, ex-'92.
W. H. Stevens, ex-'94.
C. E. Parker, '01.

ITALY.

William Burt, '81.
N. W. Clark, '83.
F. H. Wright, ex-'84.
E. E. Count, '89, returned.
A. W. Leonard, '01, returned.

JAPAN.

J. C. Davidson, '73.
Julius Soper, '73.
C. W. Green, '82, returned.
H. B. Johnson, '83.
K. Kawamura, ex-'83, deceased.
D. S. Spencer, '83.
John Weir, ex-'87, returned.

Y. Honda, ex-'92.
T. Hasegawa, '93.
H. Yamaka, '93.
Y. S. Sacon, '95.
A. D. Berry, '98.
K. Obata, '98.
T. Mine, '98.
K. Kimura, '00.
C. S. Davidson, '01.
T. Ikeda, ex-'01.
S. Kataoka, '02.
H. Kawasumi, ex-'03.
H. Kihara, ex-'03.
F. N. Scott, '99.

KOREA.

H. G. Appenzeller, '85, deceased.
W. A. Noble, '96.
W. C. Swearer, '98.
C. D. Morris, '00.
J. Z. Moore, '03.

TURKEY.

B. M. Krikorian, '91, massacred.

MALAYSIA.

S. S. Myrick, ex-'00.
B. F. Van Dyke, ex-'02.
A. J. Amery, '03.

MEXICO.

L. B. Salmáns, '83.
H. A. Bassett, '97.

PERSIA.

Rudolf Wahl, ex-'73.
Samuel Badal, '93.

PHILIPPINES.

E. P. Easterbook, '92, army chaplain.
J. C. Goodrich, '96.

W. A. Brown, '00.
Benson Baker, '03, under appointment.

PORTO RICO.

M. Andujar, '95.

URUGUAY.

F. J. Batterson, '02.

Drew Missionary Offerings.

For several years the students have annually raised certain amounts of money for some specific object, either for some one in the field in whom they have a personal interest, or to send some one out to the work. The following amounts have been thus raised by the students themselves:

1900.	To send Charles Morris to Korea,	$323.00
1901.	For Dr. T. J. Scott, Bareilly, India,	$300.00
1902.	To Charles Morris, for "The Drew House" and for salary,	$298.38
1903.	To send Saul Kataoka to Japan,	$125.00
	To J. B. Baker, J. Z. Moore, A. J. Amery,	25.00
	Total,	$150.00
1904.	For Ginza Building in Tokio, Japan,	184.75
	Total for five years,	$1,266.13

The Young Men's Christian Association of Drew Theological Seminary.

ORGANIZED 1898.

OFFICERS.

1904-1905.

President—Dr. S. F. Upham.
Vice-President—I. A. Morton.
General Secretary—W. N. Parker.
Recording Secretary—H. W. Burgan.
Treasurer—C. H. McCrea.

DIRECTORS.

FROM THE FACULTY.

Dr. S. F. Upham.
Dr. C. F. Sitterly.
Dr. J. A. Faulkner.

CLASS OF 1905.

H. R. Scott.
N. O. Sweat.
H. C. Lytle.

CLASS OF 1906.

C. W. Inglehart.
C. A. Felt.
O. H. Rey.

CLASS OF 1907.

To be elected.

COMMITTEES.

Finance—C. H. McCrea, C. H. Tobias, A. C. Flandreau.
Missionary—Dr. S. F. Upham, E. D. Soper, C. W. Iglehart.
Executive—N. O. Sweat, M. W. Beckwith.

Devotional—Dr. C. F. Sitterly, H. R. Scott, H. H. Fowler, C. L. Cole.

Social—L. H. Hough, J. V. Thompson, E. D. Soper, C. E. Ames, E. M. Compton, V. M. McCombs, H. G. Humphrey.

Lecture—Dr. J. A. Faulkner, W. R. Moyer, H. L. Smith.

Athletic—H. C. Lytle, C. W. Williams, W. W. Sweet, W. I. Dice.

Hand-book—G. P. Dougherty, W. M. Nesbit, E. W. Byshe, W. S. Jackson.

Music—C. A. Gilbert, R. S. Boyce, T. B. Young, A. N. Smith.

Self Help—S. G. Ayres, E. E. Hart, J. S. Carroll.

Auditing—N. P. Champlin, H. E Bright, D. N. Lacy.

Constitution.

ARTICLE I.—NAME.

The name of this association shall be "The Young Men's Christian Association of Drew Theological Seminary.

ARTICLE II.—OBJECT.

The object of this association shall be: (1) to deepen the spiritual life of the students; (2) to promote interest in and consecration to the cause of missions—city, home, and foreign; (3) to bring the students of the Seminary into organic relation with the World's Students' Christian Federation.

ARTICLE III.—Membership.

Every student of the Seminary shall be *ipso facto* a member of the association. Members of the faculty shall be *ex-officio* members of the association.

ARTICLE IV.—Officers.

The officers of this association shall consist of a board of directors, who shall elect their officers as hereinafter provided.

Sec. 2. The annual election shall be on the last Wednesday of February, at which time shall be chosen by ballot at large three directors from the incoming Senior and Middle classes; at a convenient time the Faculty also shall elect three of their number as directors of the association. These directors shall hold office for one year, and shall enter office upon the third Tuesday of March following. Upon the last Wednesday in October, the junior class shall elect three of their number to be members of the board of directors. They shall enter office immediately after election and hold office for the term named, or until their successors shall have entered upon the discharge of their duties.

Sec. 3. The board of directors shall at their meeting on the third Wednesday of March, elect by ballot a member of the faculty to be president, one of the students to be vice-president, another to be treasurer, another to be recording secretary, one from the incoming senior class to be general secretary, and one from the incoming senior class, other than the treasurer, to be chairman of the auditing committee, said officers to hold office for one year, or until their successors are elected and have entered upon the discharge of their duties.

SEC. 4. The president shall preside at all business meetings and all other meetings when the committee has not especially arranged for a presiding officer. He shall appoint the standing committees for his term of office, and with the help of the general secretary shall organize them at once upon entering office. He shall at the close of each term of office present a written report covering the work of the year and shall present recommendations for the future work of the association.

SEC. 5. The vice-president shall perform the duties of the president in the absence of the latter.

SEC. 6. The recording secretary shall keep the minutes of all meetings of the board and the association.

SEC. 7. The general secretary shall be the executive officer, under the direction of the board of directors. He shall conduct the correspondence of the association, and shall present a written report of the work of the monthly meeting of the board to the student body at the chapel meeting following the regular meeting of the directors. He shall have general oversight of all the work of the association and shall, in connection with the several committees, devise new plans for enlarging the scope of the association work.

SEC. 8. The treasurer shall be the custodian of all the funds of the association and shall be *ex-officio* chairman of the finance committee. He shall keep a complete account of the receipts and expenditures of the association and present a written report at the close of each term to the student body and at the close of his term of office.

SEC. 9. The general auditor shall, in connection with his committee composed of two members besides himself, audit all the accounts of the association at least twice each year, at the close of the term of office and at the end of the year; and shall present a report of such auditing to the association—these reports to be kept on file by the treasurer.

SEC. 10. The board of directors, through the general secretary, shall have the general supervision and control of the work, policy, and finances of the association in all of its detail. For the purpose of such supervision the board shall hold a meeting on the second Wednesday of each month.

ARTICLE V.—COMMITTEES.

SEC. 1. The Finance Committee. It shall secure funds for the current expenses of the association. It shall consist of one member from each class in addition to the treasurer of the association, who shall be chairman *ex-officio*. At the beginning of each seminary year the remaining members shall nominate a member from the incoming junior class, subect to the approval of the board of directors.

SEC. 2. The Missionary Committee. It shall be especially responsible for the development of the missionary interests of the seminary. The committee shall consist of four members, the chairman, who shall be a member of the Faculty, and one member from each class. At the beginning of each seminary year, the remaining members shall nominate one man from the junior class, subject to the ratification of the board of directors. It shall have control of the collection and disbursement of all missionary funds secured from the student body. All funds thus collected to be deposited with the association treasurer and all disbursements therefrom to be made only upon the written order of the board of directors, and shall present for filing an approved written report of all moneys collected and distributed by it during its term of office.

SEC. 3. The Student Executive Committee shall look after the necessary details of student life in the seminary, such as the ringing of the rising bell, the furnishing of papers for the reading room, the drawing for rooms in the dormitories, etc. It shall consist of one member from each class, the senior member to be chairman.

SEC. 4. The Devotional Committee, whose chairman shall be a member of the Faculty, shall have charge of all the devotional meetings of the association, providing leaders therefor and having general oversight of the spiritual welfare of the association.

Sec. 5. The Social Committee shall have charge of the social interests of the association. It shall arrange for the reception of new students and for the various functions of the Seminary year. Providing ushers for public events and having special care of the fraternal spirit of the association.

Sec. 6. The Lecture Committee shall be composed of one member from each of the two upper classes, with a member of the Faculty as chairman. It shall provide for the lectures and addresses given under the auspices of the association.

Sec. 7· The Athletic Committee shall have charge of the athletic interests of the seminary. It shall keep the grounds in condition for the various games, and shall have charge of all tournaments, etc. It shall file approved written reports of all expenditures with the treasurer at the close of its term of office.

Sec. 8. The Hand-book Committee shall publish the annual book of general interest and information, and shall present to the association a written report, together with any balance it may have over and above the expense of publication.

Sec. 9. The Music Committee shall work under the direction of the instructor of music and shall have charge of the music for all public meetings. It shall keep the musical instruments in good order, and shall, if possible, provide a chorister or choir, or both, for daily chapel service.

SEC. 10. The Self-help Committee shall be composed of one member from each class, with a member of the Faculty who shall be the chairman. It shall keep in touch with all possible means of self-help and shall keep a register of all those desiring employment. It shall aid as large a number of students as possible.

SEC. 11. It shall further be the duty of each chairman of each committee, to present to the students at the close of each year a written report of the work done by his committee during the year, and each chairman shall place in the hands of the treasurer an approved report of all moneys received and expended by his committee during the year. All such reports to be kept on file by the treasurer.

ARTICLE VI.—MEETINGS.

SEC. 1. At the beginning of each seminary year, and as often thereafter as may seem desirable, the board of directors shall meet with the chairman of all regular committees to discuss and map out the policy and work of each committee for the ensuing year.

SEC. 2. There shall be at least one missionary meeting each month.

SEC. 3. One sixth of the membership of the association shall constitute a quorum.

ARTICLE VII.—THE VOLUNTEER BAND.

The election of the officers of the Volunteer Band shall be subject to the ratification of the board of directors. The Volunteer Band shall have full charge of its own distinctive work, but shall coöperate with the missionary committee in the foreign missionary work of the association.

ARTICLE VIII.—AMENDMENTS.

Amendments to the constitution will require two weeks' notice and a two-thirds vote of the members present: except that this article and Article I shall not be altered or repealed without the concurrence of the International Committee of the Young Men's Christian Association.

Report of Y. M. C. A. Treasurer

FOR THE YEAR ENDING MARCH 17, 1904.

RECEIPTS.

Balance from former treasurer,	$44.00
Dues to March 17, 1904,	175.75
Student missionary collection,	67.00
	$286.75

DISBURSEMENTS.

Ringing rising bell,	$35.00
Athletics,	36.73
Convention expenses,	1.98
Lectures,	50.00
Reception,	49.97
Piano tuning and repair,	11.00
Daily papers,	7.20
Balance on hand-book, '00-'01,	19.00
Hall directory,	2.00
Sundries,	4.65
Student missionary collection,	67.00
(Paid to Dr. Faulks.)	
Balance in treasury,	2.22
	$286.75

W. B. WEST,
Treasurer.

Devotional Meetings.

Each Sunday at 9 a. m., a devotional service is held under the auspices of the Y. M. C. A. in the parlors of Hoyt-Bowne Hall, conducted by a leader chosen from the faculty or the student body.

On Wednesday at 6:30 p. m., Dr. Upham leads the regular mid-week prayer-meeting in the "Old Chapel" in Mead Hall,—the wonderful meeting so dear to every Drew man, the center of inspiration of the seminary life.

Once a week are held the class prayer-meetings, where the men hold heart-to-heart converse with their classmates and enjoy sweet communion with God.

All these services are a great source of blessing, and men whose religious life has become cold and formal are revived in them. Any one who fears for the spiritual life of the rising generation of preachers should attend a few of them.

Chapel Preachers.

On Wednesday morning of each week during the school year an hour is devoted to preaching service. A member of the senior class, previously chosen, conducts the service.

On the last Wednesday of February the sacrament of the Lord's Supper is administered by the faculty, the senior class communing in a body.

The following is the list of preachers from the senior class:

      1904.   Nov. 2. Ames.
Mar. 2. Bright.   9. Faust.
    9. Clymer.   16. Lytle.
   16. Nesbit.   30. Soper.
   23. Hauger. Dec. 7. McMinn.
   30. Rhinesmith. 14. Hill.
Apr. 6. Beery.   1905.
   13. Byshe. Jan. 4. Lesh.
Sept. 21. Dougherty. 11. Tobias.
   28. Sweat.   18. Goeller.
Oct. 5. Scott, H. R. 25. Boyce.
   12. Moyer. Feb. 1. Deming.
   19. Garrison.   8. Young.
   26. Bartley.   15. Parker.

Lectures and Addresses.

1903-1904.

Rev. Robert W. Rogers, D. D., Matriculation Day Address, "Babel and Bible, a New Biblical Controversy."

Rev. Henry A. Buttz, D. D., "Contributions of Mount Sinai to New Testament Criticism."

Prof. James Orr, D. D., "Ritschlianism."

Rev. James M. Buckley, D. D., "Unchristian, Antichristian, and Christian Socialism."

Mary Harriott Norris, "Troubadours."

Rev. S. W. Dike, D. D., "Our American Problem of the Family."

Rev. T. B. Neely, D. D., "The Sunday-school."

Prof. Livingston Barbour, "Public Speaking" (two lectures).

Rev. W. F. McDowell, D. D., "The Outlook for the Ministry."

Rev. W. P. Thirkield, D. D., "The Personality and Message of the Minister."

Rev. Mark Guy Pearse, "The Business of Religion."

Dean Joseph French Johnson, "Principles of Business for the Ministry."

LECTURES ON APPLIED CHRISTIANITY ON THE JAMES W. PEARSALL FOUNDATION AT THE NEW YORK SETTLEMENT.

Mr. Jacob A. Riis, Founders' Day Address, "Tony's Hardships."

Rev. James M. Buckley, D. D., "Unchristian, Antichristian, and Christian Socialism."

Rev. S. F. Upham, D. D., "Organization for Christian Work."

Rev. S. W. Dike, D. D., "Our American Problem of the Family."

Prof. Robert W. Rogers, D. D., "The Latest News of Abraham's Age."

Bishop E. G. Andrews, D. D., "Conduct of Public Worship."

Prof. C. F. Sitterly, S. T. D., "Jerusalem and Round About."

Rev. Mark Guy Pearse, "Some Old Folks at Home."

Rev. J. A. Faulkner, D. D., "How the Early Church Met the Problem of Poverty."

BEFORE THE MISSIONARY SOCIETY.

Rev. G. F. Arms, "Missions in South America."

Rev. Homer Eaton, D. D., "Missions in the Orient."

Rev. D. S. Spencer, D. D., "Russia and Japan."

BEFORE THE STUDENTS' ASSOCIATION.

Prof. A. C. Flick, Ph. D., "Historical Aspects of Christianity.

Rev. Oscar C. Severson, D. D., "The Battle of Gettysburg."

SERMONS.

Rev. Henry A. Buttz, D. D., Baccalaureate Sermon.

Rev. S. F. Upham, D. D., Faculty Sermon, "John Wesley."

Rev. F. Mason North, D. D., Day of Prayer for Colleges, "Personality."

Rev. John A. Faulkner, D. D., Sacramental Sermon, "The Meaning of the Lord's Supper."

Fellowships, 1904-1905.

Staley Franklin Davis, B. S. Ohio Wesleyan University.

U. S. Grant Perkins, A. B. Union College.

The George R. Crooks Prize awarded to B. H. McCoy.

Student Charges.

Every year a large number of Drew men take upon themselves the duties of the pastorate in addition to their regular work at the seminary. These student-pastors achieve surprisingly large results in the advancement of Christ's kingdom. The field for such work is in the smaller towns in and about New York city. Several Drew men are assistant pastors in Metropolitan churches.

The Drew Seminary Quartette.

First Tenor—T. B. Young.
Second Tenor—R. S. Boyce.
First Bass—C. S. Black.
Second Bass—C. E. Collerd.

The work of the quartette for the year was especially that of singing the Gospel.

The quartette assisted in evangelistic services at a number of places in the vicinity of Drew, and gave several concerts, as well as rendered music for the special services at the seminary during the year.

Athletics.

Every normal student feels the need of physical exercise, and, in a moderate way, provision has been made to meet this need at Drew.

A large field affords ample room for baseball and football. Two tennis courts offer opportunities along this line, and excellent roads in every direction are a strong inducement to the bicycle rider.

The interclass baseball games and annual tennis tournaments are a source of much pleasure both to players and spectators.

The general oversight of the athletics of the seminary, care of the grounds, etc., is in charge of the athletic committee of the Y. M. C. A.

Self Help.

So great are the opportunities for self help at Drew, that by far the larger part of the students make their own way in whole or in part.

Over 100 students during the past year have been self supporting. Most of these have pastoral charges, but many others as library assistants, choristers in nearby churches, waiters in the dining hall, stenographers and typewriters, laundry agents, and in other ways have been enabled to make their expenses.

General Information.

The President's Office,—First floor in Mead Hall.

The Registrar's Office,—First floor in Mead Hall.

The Faculty Bulletin board is in the Administration Building; the general Bulletin is in Hoyt-Bowne Hall. *Watch them.*

A room is provided in the basement of Asbury Hall for the storage of bicycles. Keys may be had for a deposit of 25 cents.

Drew students are admitted to the New York preachers' meeting. Sessions are held Monday morning at eleven o'clock, at the Methodist Book Concern, 150 Fifth avenue.

All the daily papers and the church magazines are to be found in the Library.

There is a piano in Hoyt-Bowne Hall for the use of students musically inclined. By arrangement of the Student Executive Committee the hours for its use are: 7 to 9 a. m.; 12 to 2 and 5 to 7 p. m.

Bring your wheel, your camera, your tennis racquet, and baseball equipment with you. You will need them.

The men who have advertised in this book are responsible business men, and friends of the seminary. They have made this publication possible, so when you buy go to them, thereby showing your appreciation. Always mention the Handbook.

Stationery, pens and pencils, notebooks, toilet articles, and all such things needed in student life may be had at the Seminary Stationery store.

The proximity of New York city makes its great library and university facilities easily accessible to students.

The Madison Public Library is free to students who present a card signed by the librarian. The hours are: 10 a m. to 6 p. m. Mondays, Wednesdays, and Fridays; 10 a. m. to 9 p. m. Tuesdays, Thursdays, and Saturdays.

During the fall term an informal reception is given the new students by the faculty and upper-classmen.

There is a student agency for laundry, both steam and domestic. Goods received Monday are returned Thursday evening.

United States Express Company's Office is in the D., L. & W. Depot.

Western Union Telegraph Company's Office is in the D., L. & W. Ticket Office.

Telephone (Pay Station) may be found in Mead Hall.

The educational advantages enjoyed by Drew men are exceptional. Through the courtesy of the trustees of Columbia University students of the seminary may receive tuition free in any department of the university. This opportunity includes either undergraduate work, or courses leading to the post-graduate degrees, including subjects in higher education from Chinese to astronomy. The courses in sociology under Prof. Giddings are especially popular. A certain amount of work taken at Columbia will be credited also at Drew, and some courses at Drew will be counted at Columbia. Similar courtesies are extended by New York University; and many students have taken advantages of them. Men doing work at either university must be approved by the Drew faculty.

Suggestions for Everybody.

Don't miss the Wednesday morning preaching service.

If you neglect your exercise your health will suffer.

Treat the tradesmen courteously—the seminary suffers for your bad manners.

Do not become so engrossed with the business of religion that you forget its bigger, sweeter side.

Most men talk too much—do you?

The new men should carefully note the "cut system" in vogue at Drew.

Be sure to visit the points of interest in and about Morristown. "Washington's headquarters" is an old colonial mansion on Morris street, and is said to contain the finest collection of Revolutionary curios in America.

Do *not* play the piano or make other noises after hours. You will disturb some one.

You are not compelled to go to chapel. But it is your loss when you cut.

Be happy—it is your duty.

Above all things "Remember Jesus Christ."

The Browning Club.
OFFICERS.

President—J. V. Thompson.
Vice-President—E. D. Soper.
Secretary-Treasurer—C. W. Iglehart.

The Browning Club at Drew was organized to meet an increasing demand for a broader intellectual and literary sympathy in the ministry of our church. The sixth year of active work has been passed, and it begins its seventh year with the hopes of its founders fully realized, and with the future a bright one. The study of Browning and of other men who like him have seen life as it is, proves not only of æsthetic benefit, but of great practical value to ministers whose life-work will be to grapple with these same problems and situations.

The club has enjoyed itself very profitably during the past year in the study of Browning's shorter poems, and of Tennyson's "In Memoriam," and Dante's "Divine Comedy." The work for next year will include an exhaustive study of Browning's "The Ring and the Book," "Saul," and the shorter poems.

In order to do more effective work

the number of the club is limited. Membership is by election from the undergraduate students of the seminary. The meetings are held on each Tuesday evening of the school year in the Y. M. C. A. social room, Mead Hall.

The Shakspere Club.

OFFICERS.

President—Norman P. Champlin.
Vice-President—Harry E. Bright.
Secretary-Treasurer—C. H. McCrea.

The Shakspere Club was organized in November, 1901. It had its birth in a desire to better understand men, and thus be able to reach them. Outside of the Bible no writer better portrays the play of the passions than does Shakspere, and no author is more quoted or more quotable.

During the past year several plays have been read, papers have been presented, and characters studied. Larger possibilities are constantly being brought within reach of the members through the books provided by the club in conjunction with the Seminary library. The meetings are held bi-weekly, and the membership is limited.

The Phi Alpha Literary Society.

OFFICERS.

President—W. M. Nesbit.
Vice-President—H. G. Humphrey.
Secretary—Geo. P. Dougherty.
Treasurer—W. R. Moyer.

The Phi Alpha Literary Society was organized in January, 1902. The purpose of its formation and the aim of its work is increased readiness of speech, conciseness of expression, depth of thought, and breadth of scholarship. To this end the society holds weekly meetings throughout the school year, at which times debates on live questions of church and state alternate with programmes designed for general literary culture.

The membership of the society is limited in number, and vacancies are filled by election and invitation.

The Young Men's Christian Association, Madison, N. J.

President—James H. McGraw.
Secretary—E. G. Randall.

The association rooms are in the center of the village, opposite the post-office. They are well maintained, and have an air of comfort and cheerfulness which makes them attractive. The hours are from 8 a. m. until 9:30 p. m. The reading-room is open to the public and is well supplied with the daily papers and the leading periodicals. The library, restricted to the use of members, contains over 1,000 well selected volumes, devoted to a variety of subjects. The gymnasium, in the charge of a competent physical director, is open three nights a week for men, and three afternoons for boys. There is a winter course of high grade entertainments, which are enthusiastically attended. The social life of the association is very vigorous and enlists the coöperation of the greater portion of Madison people. Bible classes as well as the Sunday afternoon meetings, from 4:15 to 5, are maintained with excellent results. A prospectus giving full details and cost of membership may be secured at the office.

Madison Public Library.

The Madison Public Library is the gift of Mr. D. Willis James to the people of Madison. The use of the library is entirely free to the public, both of the town and of the neighboring villages. Any one living in the vicinity of Madison is entitled to the privileges of the library by giving as reference some resident of Madison. The library was opened to the public May 31, 1900, with about 4,500 books on its shelves. Since then about 2,500 books have been added. The library is open from 10 a. m. to 6 p. m., Mondays, Wednesdays, and Fridays; and from 10 a. m. to 9 p. m., Tuesdays, Thursdays, and Saturdays. Every one is entitled to two books at a time, provided one only is fiction. Works of fiction can be retained one week, other books two weeks. A fine of two cents a day is charged for books kept over time. The students of the seminary may have the privileges of the library by having their applications signed by the librarian of Drew Theological Seminary Library. The upstairs reading-room contains about forty periodicals, monthly and weekly. The newspaper room, with the leading New York daily papers and a few magazines, is open every day in the week, except Sunday, from 7 a. m. to 10 p. m., and is free to all.

The Madison Churches.

There are six churches in Madison open to the attendance of all who are able to go.

The Methodist Episcopal church adjoins the seminary grounds, and is a true church home for the Drew men remaining in Madison over Sunday. Dr. Faulks is pastor.

There is also a strong and active Presbyterian church, a Protestant Episcopal church, an African Methodist Episcopal, an African Baptist church, and a Roman Catholic church.

Some Methodist Episcopal Churches in New York.

Calvary—C. L. Goodell; 7th avenue and 129th street.
Church of the People and Five Points

Mission—A. K. Sanford; 63 Park street.

Grace—E. S. Tipple, Drew, '86; 104th St., between Amsterdam and Columbus avenues.

Jane St.—C. W. McPherson.

Madison Ave.—W. MacMullen, Drew, '88; Madison avenue and 60th street.

Metropolitan Temple—R. Bagnell; 7th avenue and 14th street.

St. Andrew's—A. Gillies; 76th street, between Amsterdam and Columbus avenues.

St. James'—A. McRossie; Madison avenues and 126th street.

St. Paul's—G. P. Eckman, Drew, '86; West End avenue and 86th street.

Washington Square—G. E. Strobridge; 4th street, near Washington square.

Other Prominent Churches.

Brick Presbyterian—W. R. Richards; Fifth avenue, cor. 36th street.

Fifth Avenue Presbyterian—J. Ross Stevenson; Fifth avenue, cor. 55th street.

University Place Presbyterian— George Alexander; University place, cor. East 10th street.

Central Presbyterian—W. M. Smith; 220 West 57th street.

Madison Avenue Presbyterian—C. H. Parkhurst; Madison square.

Fourth Presbyterian—Pleasant Hunter, Jr.

West End Presbyterian—John Balcolm Shaw; West 105th street and Amsterdam avenue.

Old First—Howard Duffield; Fifth avenue and 12th street.
Grace Episcopal—W. R. Huntington; Broadway and 10th street.
Old Trinity—Morgan Dix; Broadway, at Wall street.
St. George's Episcopal—W. S. Rainsford; Stuyvesant square and East 16th street.
Cathedral of St. John the Divine; Morningside Heights.
Calvary Baptist—R. S. McArthur; West 57th street.
Collegiate (Fifth Avenue)—Donald Sage McKay; Fifth avenue, cor. 48th street.
Collegiate (Marble)—D. J. Burrell; Fifth avenue and 29th street.
Madison Avenue Baptist—G. C. Lorimer; Madison avenue, cor. 31st street.
Church of the Transfiguration—(The Little Church Round the Corner)— G. C. Houghton; 29th street, just east of Fifth avenue.
Church of the Ascension—Percy S. Grant; Fifth avenue and 10th street.
St. Patrick's Cathedral—Fifth avenue and 50th street.
Temple Beth-El—Fifth avenue and 76th street.
Temple Emanu-El—Fifth avenue and 43d street.

Other Places of Interest in the Metropolis.

ART GALLERIES, MUSEUMS, ETC.

American Museum of Natural History—W. 78th street, between Central

Park W. and Columbus avenue. Free (except Monday, 25 cents).

Aquarium (building formerly known as " Castle garden "), Battery Park.

Brown Botanical and Zoological Gardens—Brown Park—Third avenue Elevated R. R., to Pelham avenue.

Eden Musee—celebrated waxworks—23d St., between Broadway and Sixth avenue—50 cents.

Metropolitan Museum of Art—Central Park, Fifth avenue, and E. 82d street. Free (except Monday and Friday, 25 cents).

EDUCATIONAL INSTITUTIONS.

College of the City of New York—Lexington avenue and 23d street. Columbia University:—

Main buildings of the University, including Columbia College, the Schools of Applied Science, Law, Fine Arts, Political Science, Philosophy, and Pure Science—Morningside Heights—Amsterdam avenue to Broadway, 116th to 120th streets—Finest college library building in the country (320,000 volumes).

Barnard College—Broadway and 119th street.

Teachers' College and Horace Mann Schools—Broadway and 120th street.

College of Physicians and Surgeons —Amsterdam avenue, and 60th street.

College of Pharmacy—68th street, between Columbus avenue and Broadway. Cooper Institute, 8th street, Third and Fourth avenues.

General Theological Seminary

(Episcopal)—Chelsea Square, Ninth to Tenth avenue, 20th to 21st streets.
New York University:—

Administration offices, and Schools of Law and Pedagogy—Washington Square, East. Undergraduate School and Department of Arts and Sciences—University Heights, near Kingsbridge—Hall of Fame.

Union Theological Seminary—Fourth avenue and 69th street.

LIBRARIES.

Apprentices—18 E. 16th street—130,000 vols.

Astor—40 Lafayette Pl.—290,000.

Columbia University—Morningside Heights—320,000. Lenox—Fifth avenue and 70th street—110,000.

New York Historical Society—Second avenue and 11th street—70,000.

GENERAL SUGGESTIONS.

Of course one should visit the great financial center in Wall street and the immediate vicinity.

Battery Park is attractive because of historic associations, the fine view of the Bay, and the Barge Office and the Custom House. From here a free boat runs to the Emigrant Station at Ellis Island.

At City Hall Park are the City Hall, the Court House, the Post-office, and the homes of many great newspapers ("Newspaper Row").

Chinatown, in the neighborhood of Mott, Pell, and Doyer streets, and the Jewish Quarter about Hester street, must be seen, to be appreciated. No one should try to find dens in Chinatown without a guide. It is dangerous.

The great retail shopping district extends along Broadway from about 8th street to 34th street, on Sixth avenue from 14th street to 23d street, and across 14th and 23d streets. It may be seen in full glory in holiday times.

A trip along Fifth avenue, either on foot or in the omnibus, is full of varied interest; for here are ranged many beautiful churches, magnificent club-houses, and the splendid residences of millionaires.

Central Park is worthy of careful exploration, and a walk on Riverside Drive will be found very enjoyable.

Finally, buy a good guide-book, or better still get somebody to show you around; and don't expect to "do the town" completely in a day or a week. Take your time.

Points of Interest in Brooklyn.

Navy Yard—Flushing-avenue trolley at Brooklyn Bridge. Write commandant in advance for a pass.

Prospect Park—500 acres; Flatbush avenue car at Brooklyn Bridge.

New Museum of Brooklyn Institute of Arts and Sciences, on Eastern Parkway east of main entrance to Prospect Park. Flatbush avenue trolley at Bridge. Notice Triumphal Arch at the Park Plaza surmounted by Victory Quadriga by Macmonnies.

Coney Island—Any of the dozen lines at Bridge or ferries.

Manhattan Beach—Elevated Railway at Bridge.

Brighton Beach—Flatbush trolley at Bridge.

Forest Park.—A natural park of 540 acres. Myrtle avenue trolley at Bridge.

Mail Service.

INCOMING MAILS.

From the East.	From the West.
5:45 a. m.	8:02 a. m.
8:28 a. m.	9:48 a. m.
12.44 p. m.	1:23 p. m.
4:31 p. m.	3:23 p. m.

Allow from 10 to 20 minutes for distribution.

OUTGOING MAILS.

To the East.	To the West.
8:02 a. m.	8:28 a. m.
9:48 a. m.	12:44 p. m.
11:15 a. m.	4:31 p. m.
1:23 p. m.	
3:23 p. m.	
7:00 p. m.	

Mails close 10 minutes earlier.

CARRIER SERVICE.

Deliveries are made at the seminary at the following hours: 7:45 a. m.; 1:45 p. m.; and 5 p. m.; with a second morning delivery to the Library and Mead Hall at 9:30 a. m. Collections are made from the seminary boxes at the time of delivery.

Passenger Train Service Between New York and Madison.

Corrected to February 1, 1904.

To New York.		From New York.	
Leave Madison	Arrive New York.	Leave New York.	Arrive Madison
5.30 AM	7.20 AM	4.30 AM	6.05 AM
x6.09....	7.30...	6.00....	7.36....
6.40....	7.55....	7.10....,	8.28....
x7.00....	8.15....	8.10.....	9.31....
7.21....	8.35....	8.50....	10.04....
x7.58....	9.05....	9.30.....	10.56....
8.02....	9.15....	10.10....	11.45....
x8.32....	9.25....	11.10....	12.44 PM
8.44 ...	9.45....	12.00 N	1.16....
9.16....	10.30....	k1.20 PM	2.30....
9.30....	11.00....	2.00....	3.22....
10.19....	11.40....	x2.30....	4.04....
11.15....	12.40 PM	3.20....	4.31....
11.56....	1.20....	x4.00....	4.53....
12.50 PM	2.10....	4.00.....	5.03..,.
1.24....	2.50.....	4.30....	5.43...
2.24....	3.40....	x4.30....	6.12....
k3.05....	4.25 ..	x5.00....	6.01....
3.25....	4.40....	5.20.....	6.38....
4.32....	5.50....	5.40.....	6.47....
5.19 ...	6.40....	6.00....	7.17....
6.32....	7.55....	6.30....	8.00....
7.34....	8.55....	7.30....	8.57....
8.09....	9.25....	8.00....	9.22....
9.09....	10.25....	9.15....	10.41....
10.00....	11.25....	10 45....	12.12 AM
11.30....	12.55 AM	a12.30 AM	1.50....

a Except Monday. k Saturday only.
x Will not run on holidays.

DAILY PROGRAMME.

Hour.	Monday.	Tuesday.	Wednesday.	Thursday.	Friday.	Saturday.
7:45						
8:40		Chapel.	Preaching.	Chapel.	Chapel.	
9:00						
10:00						
11:00						
12:00						
2:00						
3:00						

SEPTEMBER.

1		T
2		F
3		S
4		S
5		M
6		T
7		W
8		T
9		F
10		S
11		S
12		M
13		T
14		W
15		T
16		F
17		S
18		S
19		M
20		T
21	RECEPTION OF CANDIDATES.	W
22	BEGINNING OF SEM. YEAR.	T
23		F
24		S
25		S
26		M
27		T
28		W
29		T
30		F

OCTOBER.

1	S
2	S
3	M
4	T
5	W
6	T
7	F
8	S
9	S
10	M
11	T
12	W
13	T
14	F
15	S
16	S
17	M
18	T
19	W
20 FOUNDERS' DAY.	T
21	F
22	S
23	S
24	M
25	T
26	W
27	T
28	F
29	S
30	S
31	M

NOVEMBER.

1		T
2		W
3		T
4		F
5		S
6		S
7		M
8	ELECTION DAY.	T
9		W
10		T
11		F
12		S
13		S
14		M
15		T
16		W
17		T
18		F
19		S
20		S
21		M
22		T
23		W
24	THANKSGIVING.	T
25		F
26		S
27		S
28		M
29		T
30		W

DECEMBER.

1		T
2		F
3		S
4		S
5		M
6		T
7		W
8		T
9		F
10		S
11		S
12		M
13		T
14		W
15		T
16		F
17	CHRISTMAS VACATION.	S
18		S
19		M
20		T
21		W
22		T
23		F
24		S
25		S
26		M
27		T
28		W
29		T
30		F
31		S

JANUARY, 1905.

1		S
2		M
3	SECOND TERM.	T
4		W
5		T
6		F
7		S
8		S
9		M
10		T
11		W
12		T
13		F
14		S
15		S
16		M
17		T
18		W
19		T
20		F
21		S
22		S
23		M
24		T
25		W
26		T
27		F
28		S
29		S
30		M
31		T

FEBRUARY.

1		W
2		T
3		F
4		S
5		S
6		M
7		T
8		W
9		T
10		F
11		S
12		S
13		M
14		T
15		W
16		T
17		F
18		S
19		S
20		M
21	SENIOR EXAMS.	T
22		W
23		T
24		F
25		S
26		S
27		M
28		T

MARCH.

1	W
2	T
3	F
4	S
5	S
6	M
7	T
8	W
9	T
10	F
11	S
12	S
13	M
14	T
15	W
16	T
17	F
18	S
19	S
20	M
21	T
22	W
23	T
24	F
25	S
26	S
27	M
28	T
29	W
30	T
31	F

APRIL.

1	S
2	S
3	M
4	T
5	W
6	T
7	F
8	S
9	S
10	M
11	T
12	W
13	T
14	F
15	S
16	S
17	M
18	T
19	W
20	T
21	F
22	S
23	S
24	M
25	T
26	W
27	T
28	F
29	S
30	S

MAY.

1		M
2		T
3		W
4		T
5		F
6		S
7		S
8		M
9		T
10		W
11		T
12		F
13		S
14	COMMENCEMENT WEEK.	S
15		M
16		T
17		W
18		T
19		F
20		S
21		S
22		M
23		T
24		W
25		T
26		F
27		S
28		S
29		M
30		T
31		W

MEMORANDA.

MEMORANDA.

MEMORANDA.

MEMORANDA.

MEMORANDA.

MEMORANDA.

MEMORANDA.

ADVERTISEMENTS.

TO THE READER.

It is only through the generosity of the advertisers in this manual that we are enabled to present it to you. For this reason we would earnestly urge the students and friends of the Seminary to patronize those merchants whose advertisements are found in this book, knowing from experience that they are reliable and worthy of your patronage.

ADVERTISEMENTS.

MEMORANDA.

DAY'S,
AT MORRISTOWN.

Caterer,

Confectioner,

Ice Cream

Dealer.

ESTABLISHED 1862.

Furnished the entertainment at the opening of Drew Seminary, 1867, and semi-annually every year since.
Still doing business at the old stand.

Your patronage is solicited.

Telephone No. 118.

W. F. DAY,
MORRISTOWN, N. J.

MEMORANDA.

Floor Pushes.   Gas Lighters.

E. P. FELCH,

General Electric Supplies,

33 Main St.,

MADISON, N. J.

Electrician to the Seminary.

Electric Light Wiring.

Bells, annunciators, burglar alarms, door springs, magneto medical machines, dynamos, and motors.

WILSON & DERVAN,

Bicycle and Electric Dealers.

Lock and gunsmiths, house wiring, bell work.

Athletic Supplies.

Satisfaction guaranteed.   'Phone 78 F.

W. P. TURNER & CO.

Clothing,
Hats,
and Furnishings

PARK PLACE AND BANK ST.

Your Patronage Solicited.

Bell Building,   MORRISTOWN, N. J.

MEMORANDA.

GO TO

BROWN'S

FOR YOUR

UP-TO-DATE STATIONERY OF ALL
GRADES AND PRICES.

OUR

SODA WATER

is the best in town.

---

*Pure Drugs and Prescriptions
a specialty.*

---

*Fine confections. Cameras and
camera supplies.*

DAILY AND WEEKLY PAPERS.

Prices guaranteed the lowest.

WILLIAM T. BROWN,

Cor. of Main Street and Waverly Place,

MADISON, NEW JERSEY.

MEMORANDA.

Seminary Stationery Store

COME FOR ANYTHING YOU WANT

Stationery, Waterman Fountain Pens, Ink, Mucilage, Desk Supplies, Athletic Goods, Toilet Articles, Photo Supplies, Drugs, Watch Repairing, Furnishings for Rooms.

CRACKERS AND CONFECTIONERY

Agent for the Regal Shoes

FIRST FLOOR OF ASBURY HALL

W. C. & L. C. PARKER,

Photographers,

KODAKS AND SUPPLIES.

25 SOUTH ST.,

MORRISTOWN, N. J.

Telephone 195 A.

MEMORANDA.

Thomas Whittaker,

PUBLISHER,

BOOKSELLER,

IMPORTER.

Books on Practical Theology a special feature.

The latest Monographs, Essays, Sermons, Outlines, Illustrations etc. A large assortment always in stock, new and second hand.

Bibles in every variety.

2 AND 3 BIBLE HOUSE,
4TH AVENUE AND 9TH STREET,
NEW YORK.

MEMORANDA.

CHAS. K. JOHNSON,

Watchmaker, Jeweler, Engraver, Optician.

20 Main Street, opp. Public Library,

MADISON.

SEMINARY SOUVENIR SPOONS.

J. F. ALLEN,

FOR SALE

Bicycles and Sundries.

Repairing promptly and neatly executed.

Any make of wheel secured at short notice.

SPORTING GOODS.

18-19 Park Ave.,   Madison, N. J.

F. E. HELM,

THE GENTLEMEN'S FURNISHER.

Monarch Shirts, Sterling Brand Linen Collars, Melville Hats, Puck and Cook Coon Cravats.

Custom tailoring a specialty. Union Steam Laundry.

58 Main St.,   Madison, N. J.

MEMORANDA.

FINE STATIONERY

Is Made a Specialty at

RUNYON'S

TENNIS RACQUETS.

BASEBALL GOODS.

FINE PICTURE FRAMING.

Runyon's Book Store,

MORRISTOWN, N. J.

NEW BOOKS

Are Found at

RUNYON'S BOOK STORE,

MORRISTOWN, N. J.

MEMORANDA.

OUR JEWELER.

For a good watch, clock, piece of jewelry, or silverware, or when your spectacles or eye glasses need repairing, go to

J. S. HALL,

The Morristown Jeweler and Optician.

14 Washington St.

CARRELL,

MORRISTOWN'S LEADING

Hatter and Furnisher.

EVERYTHING

Up=to=date at agreeably low prices.

PARK PLACE.

MEMORANDA.

PUBLICATIONS

OF

MESSRS.

A. C. ARMSTRONG & SON,

3 and 5 West 18th Street,
near 5th Avenue, NEW YORK.

Recommended by the Professors of the Seminary.

Bruce, Humiliation of Christ.
Bruce, Training of the Twelve.
Smith, Geography of the Holy Land.
Matheson, Studies of Portrait of Christ. 2 vols.
Matheson, Representative Men of the Bible.
Orr, Neglected Factors.
Dale, - Christian Doctrine.
Nicoll, The Church's One Foundation.
Denny, The Death of Christ.
Jowett, Brooks by the Traveler's Way.

The above may be obtained of

S. G. AYERS,

Seminary Library.

MEMORANDA.

Opp. Y. M. C. A.

Cleaning and pressing.

Suits made to order.

OSMUN CO.

Below New York Prices.

Clothing, Hats, Furnishings

Cut Rate Bargain House.

WEBER,

BOOTS,
SHOES,
SLIPPERS,
RUBBERS,
SHOE POLISH, etc.

The patronage of the students is solicited.

MADISON, N. J.

THE RIDGEDALE,

MADISON, N. J.

An attractive family boarding-house.

Fine Grounds and Verandas.
500 feet elevation. Stabling.

OPEN ALL THE YEAR.

MEMORANDA.

I make a specialty of equipping schools and colleges with sporting goods of all kinds.

TENNIS, GOLF AND BASEBALL GOODS.

Tennis Shoes, Red Rubber Soles, best quality, $1.50.

SCHOOL CAPS AND BANNERS

Made To Order.

VICTOR A. WISS,

23 South Street,

MORRISTOWN, N. J.

Tel. 273 R.

MEMORANDA.

Parker & Van Cleve,

SUCCESSORS TO
J. E. PARKER,

Jewelers and Opticians,

MORRISTOWN, N. J.

Tel. 342 A.

Pianos ..

RENTING, TUNING, AND REPAIRING.

Sheet Music and Musical Instruments of all kinds.

C. C. ZEEK,

Becker Block,   MORRISTOWN.

ENSMINGER'S
Photo Studio.

17 West Park Place, 2 doors from P. O.
MORRISTOWN, N. J.

Developing and Printing for Amateurs.

89

MEMORANDA.

TELEPHONES
1152
1153
MADISON SQUARE

Pfotenhauer & Nesbit

ST. JAMES BUILDING,

1133 BROADWAY,

NEW YORK.

Impervious Front Bricks, Enameled and Paving Bricks

Vitrified Roofing Tiles of every description.

The "Administration Building" at Drew is built of our Genuine New England "Harvard" Bricks.

MEMORANDA.

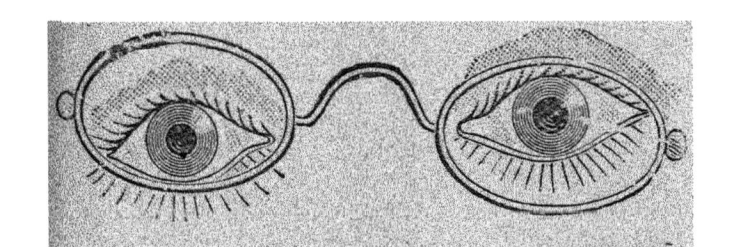

I. D. LYON,

Watches, Diamonds, Rich

Jewelry, Silverware,

McALPIN BLOCK,

MORRISTOWN, N. J.

Fine Watch Repairing.

SEMINARY

BOOK

STORE.

BOOKS FURNISHED AT LOWEST PRICES.

MEMORANDA.

MONEY AND PATIENCE

will be saved by consulting our new catalogue entitled BEST BOOKS when you select the next book worth your while to read. It contains the names of the books and their authors which are commended by the best critics on all subjects of special or general interest. A postal card request will bring it to you free of charge.

EATON & MAINS, Publishers,

150 Fifth Avenue, " " " New York.

MEMORANDA.

COUNTRY BOARD.

Large modern house, all improvements, good shady grounds, spacious verandas, 10 minutes from station, 500 feet elevation.

MAOLIS HOUSE,

78 Ridgedale Ave.,
MADISON, N. J.

W. H. KLINEDINST,

Artist and Photographer,

Waverly Place, Madison, N. J.

Branches at Morristown and Chatham.

SPECIAL RATES TO STUDENTS.

At Chatham Branch on Saturday afternoons of each week only.

VIEDT'S

Paul Zimmerman, Proprietor.

Manufacturing Confectioner,

ICE CREAM AND SODA WATER,

51 Main St.,

MADISON, N. J.

MEMORANDA.

A Postal Card will
bring me with
a fine line of goods.

Newton Ely,

DOVER, N. J.

Designer and
Maker of
Men's Clothes.

MEMORANDA.

CHARLES P. EVERITT,

123 East 23d Street,

NEW YORK.

❧

The only place in New York to buy second-hand books cheap.

J. S. PAULMIER, President.
H. I. BRITTIN, Vice-President.
FRED B. BARDON, Cashier.

The First National Bank

OF MADISON, N. J.

CAPITAL, • • $50,000.00
SURPLUS AND PROFITS, $35,732.61

DIRECTORS:

J. S. PAULMIER,
H. I. BRITTIN;
GEORGE P. COOK,
EDWARD MILLER,
CHARLES E. COOK,
FRED B. BARDON.

MEMORANDA.

BOOKS RARE, NEW, and SECOND HAND

BOUGHT FOR CASH.

Great Bargains in Fine Sets. Theological Books. Call and inspect same. Catalogues on application.

Importers of Old and Rare Books.

Everitt & Francis Co.,

116 EAST 23d STREET,

NEW YORK.

IT PAYS ME TO DO GOOD WORK

IF you have printing to do, give me a trial.
I am ready to do good work at reasonable prices.

New Type
New Presses

HAVE three thousand dollars' worth of new type and new machinery.
Estimates gladly furnished.

EDGAR C. MARKHAM,
68 MAIN ST., MADISON, N. J.

IT PAYS ME TO DO GOOD WORK

MEMORANDA.

Next to the new City Hall.

We sell everything man wears, from head to foot.

CLOTHES,
FURNISHINGS,
HATS,
SHOES.

A special discount allowed to ministers.

MARKS & BENSON CO.,

116-118 East 14th Street,

NEW YORK CITY.

Opposite Irving Place.

MEMORANDA.

HELPFUL BOOKS.

THE NEW DAY

By RUSSEL H. CONWELL, D. D. 16mo. 117 pages. Price, 50 cents net; postpaid, 56 cents.

This is a series of practical papers for young men. Doors of usefulness and of advancement are open now to them as never before. No obstacle bars their way if they are determined.

President Henry G. Weston, D. D., says: "It is full of good sense, good advice, and good feeling. I know of no book of the same number of pages that would do the mass of American young men more good."

The Bible and How to Teach It

By ALVAH HOVEY, D. D., LL. D., and J. M. GREGORY, LL. D. Price 25 cents net; postpaid, 30 cents.

No one is competent to teach the Bible until he knows what the Bible contains. The Bible addresses the intellect as well as the heart, and we can acquire a knowledge of its contents by hard study only. To all who undertake this study this little book will render essential service.

A Young Man's Difficulties with His Bible

By D. W. FAUNCE, D. D. 196 pages. Price 25 cents net; postpaid, 30 cents.

"Of the spirit and style of the book nothing need be said except in praise. The author comes to the doubter as a helper. He is never harsh or impatient. He understands young men. He wishes to treat their doubts fairly, and to show them that the grounds of faith are sufficient."—*The McMaster University Monthly.*

American Baptist Publication Society,
PHILADELPHIA.

New York House, 132 East 23d Street

MEMORANDA.

PHOENIX LAUNDRY,

Easton, Pennsylvania.

⊕

BRANCH OFFICE,

DREW THEOLOGICAL SEMINARY,

No. 30 Asbury Hall,

J. V. THOMPSON,

Agent.

⊕

Laundry collected Friday,
3 to 5 p. m.
Monday, 11 a. m. to 1 p. m.
Delivered Thursday, 5 p. m.

Lightning Source UK Ltd.
Milton Keynes UK
UKHW010013301218
334537UK00013B/1864/P